MW01701700

# The Power of Addiction and The Strength to Overcome It

## Confessions of A High-Functioning Alcoholic

By T. D. W.

Published by T. D. W. ISBN Services



ISBN: 979-8-89589-448-4

Library of Congress Control Number: 2018675309

Printed in the United States of America

# Preface

# Preface

My hope for this book, as I let you into the deepest darkest times of my life, bare my soul to you and give you the no holds bar secrets in its entirety, is for my story to have a positive impact. Whether you need help or know someone who does, my story may shed a light on the power of alcohol addiction and why * 90% of alcoholics do not maintain their sobriety. At the time I'm writing this to you, I am five and a half years sober. This story is about the strongest relationship I've ever had and how I broke up with Alcohol.

On 1/28/2019 God and Jesus bestowed on me the most valuable gifts of my life - the guidance, strength and understanding I needed to live a sober, alcohol-free life. After procrastinating on writing this book for a few years, I decided that for my story to make sense and have a real impact on you, the reader, I must be completely honest with you about my alcohol addiction and how it came about. You need to know the what, why, how and all the things that happened along the way to have a real understanding about alcohol addiction and how it took over my life. It was like I was smacked right in the face, "Ouch!" and realized **I MUST TELL YOU EVERYTHING** that happened from beginning to end for it to make sense. I'm giving you the ugly truth about alcohol addiction, the very bumpy road along the way and how it could have fucked up my life. What you are going to read in these pages are some of the most embarrassing, disappointing and unattractive choices I've made in my life. The truth is shocking and may be unbelievably disturbing, but It's my truth.

If I can influence at least one person's life, to help someone else get through their struggle, then it will all have been worth it.

**Disclaimer:** All the information in this story is based on my own personal experiences with alcohol addiction. I am not a doctor, psychiatrist, psychologist or therapist of any kind and have never claimed to be. I only hope to help others with my story.

*90% of those who enter rehab to get sober relapse and kindling occurs, making it harder to end the cycle of alcoholism.

# Dedication

# Dedication

I truly believe that God and Jesus help those who help themselves. I was praying, begging for my life to be spared and I am still here today. My weeks of alcohol withdrawals had been full of irrational thoughts, fears and feelings of pure terror. I didn't know what to do as seconds turned into minutes and minutes turned into hours and hours turned into days… Within the first couple hours of stopping "cold turkey", I began to feel the beginning stages of withdrawals. The only thing to do was to start Googling on my iPhone while in my bed drenched in sweat, trying to understand what was happening to me. I needed to know more about alcohol withdrawal symptoms, and what effects Alcohol has on your body and brain. Why am I in so much pain? How long will this last? I had a million questions...

I found all the answers I needed, thanks to God and Jesus.

My Googling led me to the website www.fit-recovery.com and a blog of articles about alcoholism that answered all my questions when I needed them the most. At the bottom of each article, other alcoholics, just like me, wrote comments about their own personal stories. It gave me the information I needed, when I needed it, just to know what was happening to me. I felt desperate needing to understand that I wasn't crazy and that there was a light at the end of the tunnel. I am not alone. The insanity that was overtaking all my thoughts and all the excruciating pain I was feeling was completely normal. It eased my mind to know it was temporary, I will feel better and I will have the ability to live a happy, full and sober life.

Chris Scott, the author of the book "Drinking Sucks!" (Amazon) and his website: www.fit-recovery.com is where I found all the answers I needed. I still call Chris every year on my sobriety birthday and thank him for saving my life.

Lastly, the legacy of my beloved Mr. Mushkins (Mushy, a 15-pound French Lop Bunny Rabbit), who licked the sweat off me for weeks (yeah, he probably got tipsy) while I was in bed during my alcohol withdrawal symptoms. He was the only one with me when I went "cold turkey" and spent weeks in bed, thinking I may die. Mushy is not with me anymore, but he had many purposes in his life and his most important purpose was how he helped me get through alcohol withdrawals, become sober and he loved me at my worst time on this earth.

# <u>An Insight Into Hell</u>

# An Insight into Hell

Every inch of me was in excruciating pain. I was drenched in sweat, shaking from head to toe, my heart felt like it might burst out of my chest, muscles were spasming randomly throughout my body. The physical, psychological, emotional and spiritual pain was agonizing and almost too much to bear. The thoughts and questions flashing through my mind were those of a completely insane person. My brain and body were slowly depleting of Alcohol and would do **ANYTHING** to obtain the poison it depended on. It was trying to trick me into taking just one sip…

"Take just one sip and you'll feel better" my brain kept telling me, if just for one second of "relief" …

# Who Can Become Addicted to Alcohol?

# Who Can Become Addicted to Alcohol?

Hi, my name is Tiffany and I'm an alcoholic. Currently, I am a 45-year-old single woman with no children of my own. I just completed my 19th year teaching Pre-K ESE. An ESE student means "exceptional student education" for students with disabilities. My class consists of 3–5-year-olds with a variety of developmental delays, speech/language impairment, physical disabilities, autism, etc. Though it is exhausting, I love teaching my "little ones" even if it is probably a big reason I never had kids of my own. I believe any desire I may have had to be a mother was satisfied in the many classes I've taught... I've had the opportunity to touch the lives of more than 350 children, not many people can say that. However, I never wanted to bring one home with me.

I grew up an only-child, a white Jewish girl in Miami. I went to an elite private college preparatory school for Middle School and my first two years of High School, Gulliver Academy and Gulliver Preparatory School. My parents and I moved to Central Florida the summer before my junior year of high school, but more about that trauma later. Then I went to college at University of Central Florida in Orlando.

Growing up I was very rarely ever exposed to Alcohol. It would have never crossed my mind to touch it. It was never a subject in my home growing up. My parents are loving, well-educated professionals who worked very hard to provide me with the kind of home they didn't grow up in. I was very sheltered and kept out of a lot of trouble that a teenager can easily stumble into.

I know how very lucky I am.

So, how can a girl who grew up like this become an alcoholic? Alcohol addiction occurs in all walks of life. It does not discriminate. It doesn't matter what gender you are, what color you are, what religion you are, how much money you make or anything else. No one is immune to the possibility of becoming addicted to Alcohol. Hey, it may not be an addiction to Alcohol but something else. Sugar, salt, gambling, pornography, smoking, even shopping can be an addiction! We're in trouble now... I didn't know or understand the gravity of my grandparent's alcohol addiction during my long and extensive drinking habit. It may be important to ask your family members what health conditions run in your family. My alcoholism showed me there is a genetic component to addiction.

One thing I've learned is that **everyone is going through something**. We may not know what it is, but we all have something to work on, whether it be an addiction, a tragedy, other health challenges, mental disorders, etc. After what I've been through, I try my best not to judge anyone for anything. If I did, I would be a hypocrite.

# Looking Back

# Looking Back

Honestly, I'm not sure how I'm still here to tell my story. I've had friends I would drink with, some of them ended up with horrible health conditions like pancreatitis (she almost died), liver problems, permanent neurological pain, numbness, pain and tingling going down their limbs and/or nonstop migraines. Writing this book and admitting my "flaw" about this subject feels risky. I've been warned to be careful. Being an alcoholic is stigmatized and continues to be a taboo subject in our society, even though it's **EVERYWHERE!**

I decided the only way to reach as many of my target audience as possible was to write directly to you and be completely honest about my frightening story of life with my "best friend" Alcohol. I loved it but I didn't realize it was using and abusing me. Alcohol had complete control of my life and my actions. I wouldn't dare leave home without it, nor did I think I could live my life without it. Be warned: the details revealed to you in these pages may shock you or you may wake up and realize this is your story, too.

See I'm one of those alcoholics considered "high-intensity" or "high-functioning" and I was a lover not a fighter. My personality and responses did not give away the fact that I was always drunk.

Most people closest to me; my family, friends, coworkers knew that I enjoyed a mixed drink of vodka, club soda and lime. No one knew I would go through a fifth of vodka and a fifth of tequila in less than a week all by myself. I would go to sleep with a shot of liquor to wake up for a shot of liquor. I drank all day long no matter where I was- home, by myself, shopping, floating in the pool, the beach, restaurants, anywhere and everywhere. I took it with me, hiding liquor in my Perrier bottles. I took risks like drinking and driving, and after four or five long years of heavy drinking, I honestly didn't care what happened to me or if I died. I was drinking so much that drinking to meet my tolerance level only stopped the shaking, sweating and gave me energy for a little while. Then I had to keep drinking more and more throughout the day, just to feel "normal". That didn't last very long and before I knew it I would need another shot just to keep up the show. None of it was normal. It was all dangerous. I could have died. I could have hurt or killed someone. I could have lost my job. I could have ________ (you name it). I was in a bad place and even at that point I did not snap out of it.

## Traumatic Events or Bad Decisions

# Traumatic Events or Bad Decisions

Usually, it takes a traumatic event that leads to an arrest or losing one's job, their spouse or custody of their children, you name it - something usually must happen to "wake you up" before an addict may accept they have a problem and stop drinking. Please don't let a DUI, a car accident, accidentally hurting yourself or someone else, losing your job, the ability to function or any other traumatic event or bad decision become the reason you choose to fight yourself for yourself and beat alcohol addiction.

My decision to quit was fortunately only a "wake-up call" because I disappointed myself and my family. I literally scared myself into sobriety. I created a dangerous situation in my home and the next day I woke up and regretted it. That story deserves its own section of this book.

If you can turn your flaw into your strength and become sober, your sobriety birthday will be your re-birth. A re-birth of your new life, a healthy, happy one, full of positive and limitless possibilities.

# High School Trauma

# High School Trauma

Okay, so we all know alcohol addiction doesn't just start that way. Like any relationship, at first it was on its best behavior. It snuck up on me during a very challenging time in my life but let's start at the beginning. Alcohol was in my house growing up, and I never considered drinking it. Being an "only child" probably kept me from being exposed to many things and I do not recall observing the adults around me drinking Alcohol. Later in life, after the worst breakup **EVER** from Alcohol I would understand the genetic component of my alcohol addiction.

When I was sixteen, the summer before my junior year of high school, my parents and I moved to Central Florida in Polk County. I went from being highly sheltered in Miami to the very opposite in the small-town of Lake Wales, FL. This was a traumatic culture shock; my once sheltered existence was shattered as I was introduced to a completely new way of life and a completely new way of thinking. This small town is part of the bible belt of Florida where abstinence is sacrament and contraception and sex are not discussed nor taught as prevention for pregnancy or STDs. This is the place where I first saw pregnant teenage girls and I remember that I was shocked to find out my new high school had a portable building used for babysitting while their teenage moms went to class. This is the place where I was introduced to interracial dating and eventually my first experience with Alcohol.

It wasn't until I was seventeen that I tried drinking Alcohol for the first time. I remember being at a friend's house there were four of us and someone came up with a great idea! We sat in a circle and went around taking sips of Goldschläger Liquor. The gold flakes at the bottom of the bottle looked so alluring! It was my first time trying any alcohol and I felt butterflies in my tummy knowing I was about to do something I shouldn't do. The excitement of the beautiful gold flakes along with knowing I was being a bit naughty gave me a boost of courage. When it was my turn, I grasped the bottle as it was handed to me, and I couldn't wait to take a sip! I didn't just take a sip; I took a big swig of the strong scented cinnamon liquid in that bottle. Almost instantly I felt a warm feeling rush throughout my entire body and straight to my head! It would be a few years before I drank Alcohol again...

## **College Fun, Almost 21!**

# College Fun, Almost 21!

It wouldn't be until I was almost 21 years old that I would drink Alcohol again. Fast forward to my junior year in college, I couldn't wait for Rush Week to hopefully join the sorority I really wanted to be a part of. I waited patiently until it arrived... Finally, it was University of Central Florida's (UCF) Rush Week, and I went from sorority house to sorority house meeting all the girls and my possible future sisters. Kappa Delta was my dream sorority and Alcohol never entered my mind. Remember, I was a clean cut, sheltered, Jewish girl from Miami. My young twenty-year-old mind was still naïve. I was super thrilled when Kappa Delta asked me to join them as their sister! It was the beginning of a wonderful sisterhood experience and the start of my Alcohol drinking career. As my sisters and I went together to different social events, there it was, Alcohol, (my future nemesis) and I was about to turn 21, so why not? Remember, alcohol addiction doesn't just start that way…

So yes, I experienced Alcohol my junior and senior years of college, but I was in control of how much I drank. I would have one or two drinks and I could stop, find the "sisters" I came to the party with, and we would leave together just as we arrived. We never left a sister behind. We always left the event with whoever we came with and that kept us safe and accountable for each other. Joining Kappa Delta was one of the best decisions I made in college. My parents were only an hour away in Lake Wales, a place I was happy to get away from.

# **Three Lifetimes Ago…**

# Three Lifetimes Ago…

We were too young to understand what we were doing. A few years after college, when I was 25 years old, I married the guy I had been dating for a few years. He was a Jehovah's Witness and was shunned by his family and others for making choices that were not what he was taught to do according to his faith. Yes, the Jewish girl married a Jehovah's Witness and that was not my best decision, but it was not my worst. The only beautiful things to come from that three-year marriage was a beautiful wedding day on a cruise ship and the day I left him. That three years of "marriage" ended with a keg in the garage and a "husband" who couldn't seem to stop purchasing cocaine from the neighborhood junkie. Remember, broken relationships don't start that way. After being exposed to cocaine and ecstasy during a vacation to Jamaica, my ex-husband was completely hooked. Those beautiful blue eyes I once melted into became frightening, angry eyes when he would use cocaine and drink from the keg. Eventually, I was coming home from teaching to find a new eight ball of cocaine on the coffee table. Those frightening, angry eyes and the man I loved who wore them, was completely addicted to cocaine and became physically abusive. So, I left him. In hindsight I should have thought, hey now you know what addiction looks like, don't let it happen to you.

No one ever asks to be an addict.

At the end of this chapter, I was 28 years old, living back home with my parents (who now lived in Kissimmee, FL) and I continued teaching "my little ones".

## Two Lifetimes Ago…

# Two Lifetimes Ago...

One night, I met a couple of my girlfriends at The Blue Martini in Orlando for a night of dancing and drinking. I had not been single for long. We were having a great time dancing. I was still in control of my relationship with Alcohol. That night at "Blue" I met the next man who would forever alter the course of my life, for the bad and the good. This relationship lasted for about thirteen years. For anonymity I will call him J.

As we know, when you first meet someone, they show you their best side, what they want you to see. J was intelligent, attractive, co-owned a very lucrative business with his mother and a couple years into our relationship he bought a beautiful home for us to live in. At least, that's what I thought.

After dating a while, we visited his mother who lived in Miami. She was very well off and had a large estate in a ritzy community of my old hometown in Miami. It felt like fate. J and I were meant to be together. He and I would visit his mom in Miami for different holidays during our first five or so years together. Everything seemed to be lovely.

I began studying the Bible, The Old Testament (my Jewish roots) and The New Testament (where I found Christianity). I strengthened my relationship with God and accepted Jesus, being baptized as a Christian when I was about 32 years old.

In the beginning of our relationship, J seemed very attracted to me. Eventually, our intimacy left much to be desired, and I should have paid attention to the red flags that were popping up everywhere. I was so invested in our relationship by this point, I let myself accept a subpar intimate relationship. None of my personal needs were being met. Before I knew it, we were in this long-term relationship. We had our first French Lop Bunny Rabbit, Mr. Chubbles, for a few years and when he was about to turn seven and getting older, we brought another French Lop Bunny Rabbit home, Mushy.

Mr. Chubbles raised Mushy. I would bring the bunnies to my class at school, and they quickly became the school's mascots. That's about the time J's mother decided to move from Miami to about fifteen minutes away from us in Kissimmee and close to their business that J was successfully managing.

A few years later when I was about 35 years old, my relationship with J started to get well, complicated. His mother bought a house in the same neighborhood as my parents, close by. The only difference was that my parents have never been intrusive, my new "smother-in-law" most definitely was overly intrusive. It wasn't until J's mother moved nearby that I found myself the third wheel in my relationship with J. He was the daughter she never had (but wanted) and somehow our "much to be desired" intimacy became nonexistent. The years were flying by, and my memories were hazy as my drinking began to drown me. Eventually due to a medical illness, his mother moved into our house. Things continued to get stranger and stranger between the two of them. I found them sitting at the kitchen table talking shit about people. They would air out their dirty laundry, having nasty conversations about whoever was upsetting them at the time. It was weird how they would just sit at that table and go on for hours about that person, their new target. He bathed in her bathtub with the door open. She was redecorating our house. Things felt, well, weird and continued to get weirder. The weirder things got the more I was drinking.

A part of me died when Mr. Chubbles died. He waited until I left the room. That was one of the hardest days of my life. Thank goodness I still had a part of him in Mushy. Too many traumatic things had happened to me at the same time. Mr. Chubbles passed away, my two best girlfriends both moved away to different states with their families, and I found myself in a three's-a-crowd relationship with an in-the-closet gay man who was more in love with his mother than he was with me.

See, I had an extremely serious problem. I was a high-functioning, no-one-knew-but-me, alcoholic. I had been drinking Alcohol heavily anywhere and everywhere for almost five years. I know what caused my Alcohol consumption to increase and I became an alcoholic who was so reckless and dangerous, even though it took a while to understand it. It was my way of **coping** with the death of Mr. Chubbles, my two best friends moving out of state at the same time, and I was stuck in a sexless relationship for eight years at that point, with my ex who should have just gone ahead and married his mother. It was an awful situation to be in. So how did I cope? I drank a lot of Alcohol. I numbed myself so I didn't have to hurt, be sad or feel anything. It worked for a while until Alcohol consumed all of me and my life.

Of course, I can't blame anyone but myself and I don't. No one forced me to chug that tequila and bite that juicy orange slice dipped in cinnamon. That was all me. I'm the only one who purchased liquor at the store, hid it around the house, took it with me wherever I went. Do you know they have tampon flasks? No one is to blame for my alcohol abuse but me. I just know now it was my way of coping with sadness, anger, a broken heart and a broken relationship.

If it wouldn't be sold where I was going, I brought it with me. My choice of poison was tequila and vodka. I would buy a bottle of both and by the end of the week, I had gone through both bottles all by myself and this cycle would repeat, every week for about four to five years. Eventually, I would go to sleep with a shot of liquor to wake up for a shot of liquor. I put it in my Perrier bottles and brought it with me **EVERYWHERE**. Towards the end of my tumultuous drinking career this feeling of being totally drunk was my "normal". To stop the sweating, the shaking, the pain, and not pass out or throw up, **I had to drink**. I drank Alcohol in droves. I didn't care if I killed myself or if I died. That's how low it had become from the age of 35 until I turned 40.

At the time I was 35 years old, I would end up staying in this relationship with J for another five years. In that time his mother was healthy again but refused to move out of our house. I was terribly unhappy and crushed emotionally for so many reasons, drinking Alcohol became my way of handling everything happening and crashing down around me.

# Huh, What Problem?

# Huh, What Problem?

My 40th birthday “present” was a big dose of wtf reality. It taught me that I make dangerous decisions when drinking Alcohol, that I have a problem and I needed to get sober. Before the “wake-up” call and my sobriety could take place, I had half-heartedly “tried” to get sober by tapering my Alcohol consumption, but I wasn’t doing it for me. I really didn’t think I had a problem. Sobriety can only be achieved by the alcoholic’s realization of their addiction and their ability to change their mindset. Sobriety doesn’t come from how much willpower one has. Instead, it is the decisive choice to live an alcohol-free life. Alcohol must no longer be an option. Let me explain the depth of my alcohol addiction…

I told you already that I was a completely functional, no-one-knew but me alcoholic with a sweeter disposition than if I was sober. No one around me saw the extent to which my need for Alcohol had become. I would go to sleep with a shot of my favorite poison (vodka or tequila) to wake up for a shot. I didn't care if I drank and drove. I didn't care if something happened to me if I hurt myself or died. In that condition, I couldn't think far enough ahead to even imagine I could hurt someone else. The last few years in my relationship with J, I had been taking Alcohol with me **everywhere** whether it was supposed to be there or not. I would pour vodka or tequila in my Perrier bottles, take them with me, and hide bottles of Alcohol around the house. **I could not imagine my life without it.** It was the only "normal-me" that I knew anymore. After years of alcohol abuse, my brain, my body and I didn't know a life without it. It was scary to wake up and realize the scope of my alcohol addiction. Usually there is some kind of wake-up call; a DUI, a car accident, being fired from one's job, relationship problems or something dramatic to open one's eyes to the reality that they have a problem. Years flew by and I had no memories to account for them. For years of my life, I was in an alcohol-induced haze and woke up to find I had very little to no recollection of much of anything that had happened for a few years. I was coping with life's stresses by chugging Alcohol and losing time, precious time. At the end of my drinking life, I was only alive by the grace of God. It could have gone very differently, and I am very grateful.

# My Wakeup Call

# My Wakeup Call

This is not an easy story to tell, let alone write it out for everyone to read but that's how important it is to understand the gravity of alcohol addiction. Here's the completely honest, nail biting, dangerous and destructive event that happened on my 40th birthday, January 19, 2019. J and his mother were out of town for a few weeks. I had a girlfriend come stay the weekend with Mushy and I. Mr. Chubbles had passed away about five years earlier and Mushy was the French Lop Bunny Mr. Chubbles had raised, giving me a connection to Mr. Chubbles that I most certainly needed.

That 40th birthday weekend changed the trajectory of my life.

My girlfriend, for anonymity I'll call her S, came to visit and spend the weekend with me for my birthday. It was just my friend S, Mushy and I. I figured we would have a spa day, come home, order pizza and do facial masks. You know, girl stuff. I had no idea the extremely dangerous event that I would allow to take place later that night. We took shots of liquor and had a few drinks before we left for the spa. S and I went to a nail salon for pedicures. She had driven us to the nail salon only a few miles from my house. On the way back, she changed our plans and said she wanted to take me out for a birthday dinner. So we went to a local restaurant, again only a couple of miles from my house. We ate outside on the patio because S likes to smoke cigarettes, something she said she only does when she's drinking.

The next thing I knew she invited this random guy who was about to walk into the restaurant to sit next to her at our table. After some mindless chatter, S asked this stranger if he could get cocaine for us. He said "sure" and made a phone call. I was shocked and confused by her request. She and I had never talked about cocaine before or ever doing it. But "what the hell, it's your 40th birthday! Let's celebrate!" she said. I can't say I wasn't excited at the idea of doing coke with my friend on my birthday, so I went all in with my drunk self!

S drove this guy (I don't remember his name) and I to pick up the "white lady" from his friend's house. Now there's two guys, my friend S and I going back to my house to snort cocaine and drink heavily. Shit, we hadn't stopped drinking since before the shots we took at my house before the pedicures! It was my favorite shot; an orange slice dipped in cinnamon with a shot (or make it a double) of chilled tequila.

Next thing I know, the four of us are at my house enjoying the liquor (tequila or vodka, what's your poison?) and snorting the lines of white powder served on a glass plate with a rolled-up dollar bill. Heck yeah, we had fun, music blasting, drinking, drugging and dancing!

S and I were very lucky that night. God must have been shielding us from total disaster! The two random guys who came to my house were not total scum looking to rape or in any way hurt the two idiots (us) wanting to drink and get high.

The next morning, I woke up with S sleeping next to me in bed, our clothes still on from the night before. I ran around the house in complete panic, looking for him, and luckily found Mushy safe and sound; the two guys were gone. That's when I started to cry. Uncontrollable crying as I realized what a risky situation I had put S, Mushy and myself in. I couldn't believe these two guys now knew where I lived! J and his mother wouldn't be back for a couple weeks. What if these guys came back and it was just me at the house? I was so disappointed in myself and scared, so aware of the danger that could have happened, it was at that point I realized, **I DON'T MAKE GOOD DECISIONS WHEN I DRINK**. It was like a light switch flipped and the lightbulb turned on. I needed to make sure nothing like this would ever happen again!

I called my mom first thing after S left to go home. I cried hysterically as I told her everything that had happened the night before and what kind of danger I had put us in.

This situation was my eye opener, my wake-up call, my second chance at living a real, sober, healthy life with real happiness and the opportunity to make new memories that I could actually remember.

42

# The Day I Went Cold Turkey

# The Day I Went Cold Turkey

There's nothing more amazing than turning your biggest flaw into your ultimate strength. January 28, 2019, was the day I turned my life around, stopped drinking Alcohol and went cold turkey. I began the months-long excruciatingly painful fight for my life. Now 5+ years later I am in total control of my life without the desire for Alcohol. I feel empowered knowing I have the ability and the confidence to say "no!" to Alcohol. The decision has already been made and it's incredible to know Alcohol will never be an option for me again. It was a spiritual experience I had while going through withdrawals but more on that later. For now, let's rewind...

I've always believed in the saying that "God helps those who help themselves." I give all the glory to God and Jesus for helping me, leading me to the information I needed and was searching for at the exact time I was looking for it. I could never have achieved sobriety without the love and guidance of our Heavenly Father.

I was home alone for a few weeks, splashing in a puddle of my own sweat as the alcohol withdrawals, that are too painful to really describe, with only Mushy by my side. I had to make my own decision to live a sober life and I had to suffer through the immense torture to understand just how low I had gotten. There really are no words to describe just how terrifying and agonizing it felt. Nothing will ever be harder than "breaking up" with Alcohol. I was so scared and in so much pain during Alcohol withdrawals... I didn't know who I was without it.

This is what I call **The Mind Fuck**; what the starving-for-Alcohol brain is willing say to you to get you to drink.

I was thinking in a loop of insecurities, being asked frightening questions that I had no answers to, it was very confusing and terrifying:

**Who** am I without Alcohol? (Questioning my self-worth.)

**What** am I going to do if I can't drink Alcohol? (Learn to enjoy places sober and write this book to help you.)

**Where** can I go that will not have Alcohol? (Almost **EVERY** place you go serves Alcohol. Most restaurants, social gathering places, theme parks, etc. offer and encourage drinking Alcohol.)

**When** will the pain go away? (I need to understand the physical, psychological, spiritual, and emotional torture that I'm going through and how long this will last.)

**Why** on earth is this my flaw? (Of everything that I could be addicted to, why Alcohol, my BFF? It felt like the worst punishment ever!)

**Will** I still have friends? (Not drinking buddies but real friends.)

**Will** I still have fun? (I couldn't imagine my life without it.)

**How** am I going to conquer this? (You mean never have even a sip of Alcohol again? Never! How?)

My memories were very fuzzy, I didn't have many memories and those I did have included Alcohol. I didn't know what I was going to do. This was the first 24 hours being sober and it was a total freakout! I knew myself well enough to know that tapering down Alcohol daily would not work for me. I'm a use it or lose it type of girl. I got up and out of bed, angry and frustrated, on a mission to find all the liquor in the house. In a moment of pure rage, I ran around the house, angrily stomping about and found all the Alcohol! Every bit of Alcohol in the house, every liquor bottle, every Perrier bottle, every 2-ounce shot bottle. I even found all the Alcohol I had hidden around the house. I got it all together, brought it to the kitchen and I did the **unthinkable**! I poured it all down the sink! In a fit of fury and deep regret about what I had allowed to happen when I put my girlfriend S, Mushy and I in so much danger!

The next 48-72 hours were even worse. I got the "if you just take a sip of Alcohol, you'll feel so much better. Just a sip. Just. One. Sip. Please???" My body was telling my brain and my brain was begging me for just a sip... "you'll feel so much better if you just take a sip." It was as though I was three separate beings trying to fight myself for myself! My body, my brain and I were at war with each other over Alcohol! I cannot describe the magnitude of physical, emotional, psychological and spiritual pain I felt at that time. What could I do sweating, shaking, terrified with all these crazy, insane thoughts?

I went on Google. I was looking for any and all information I could find about Alcohol. I needed to know that I was not going crazy! Why did I have these insanely scary thoughts and questions? How long should this shit last? Is this normal?

Well, God helps those who help themselves, remember? I know it. That's how I found the website with the blog on all things Alcohol. I found all my answers there. At the bottom of each article, there were comments by people, just like me, who were going through sobriety or were looking back at their completely unbelievably painful experience and sharing it with others, sharing it with me! God led me to what I needed at the exact moment I needed it. The website's creator, Chris Scott, wrote a book, "Drinking Sucks!" (You can find it on Amazon) and it was his website www.Fit-Recovery.com with the blog of articles. In his book, Chris explains how Alcohol affects the brain and body. He explains which vitamins, supplements and herbs he found helped to calm his alcohol withdrawal symptoms. Maybe they could calm my severe anxiety, unbelievable depression, racing heart wanting to burst out of my chest, body aches, fear, severe sweating, my entire body shaking, numbness and tingling throughout my arms and legs and other excruciatingly painful phenomena... So, I did what anyone in my obscenely torturous position would do... I ordered every vitamin, supplement, and herb in his book to help me get through my alcohol withdrawal symptoms. They did help! They helped to ease my withdrawal symptoms, from all the chemistry damage done to my brain and body that Alcohol and I had caused.

There is a spiritual war going on around us. This is where, at about 5 days or so into quitting cold turkey, the real fight for my life was about to begin. At this point I was literally swimming in my own sweat in bed. That's when the angel and the demon showed themselves to me. They began fighting for control over me. There was an angel on my right shoulder and a demon on my left shoulder. It lasted for about an hour, their fight for my life. During that time, they were yelling at me, they were yelling at each other! The demon was screaming at me, "just go get a drink" and the angel was screaming back, "no, don't drink"! Those two went on and on yelling at me to decide! "Just take a drink!" yelled the demon! "No, don't!" screamed the angel! Back and forth, over and over, until I was in full panic mode! Honestly, until that horrifying ordeal with those two, I wasn't confidently sure what I would do. I wasn't confident about anything. They continued their full-on fight for my life and as the seconds turned into minutes it became more and more terrifying. I was uncertain about what I would do. It felt worse than any panic attack I've ever had. It was as real as real can be. I know what I heard! I know what I felt and went through, and the spiritual war went on… it continued for about an hour! They made me decide. They forced me to make the hardest decision of my life because they were fighting for mine! I screamed out "**NO!**" … It was then that those two went away, never to be seen or heard from again. They took with them my urge to drink. I was finally in the clear. I just needed to keep on going, suffering through it but now I could see the light at the end of this dark, painful tunnel.

I understand it from the alcoholic's perspective. Choosing to stop drinking caused me the most extreme levels of pain; physically, emotionally, spiritually, psychologically, in every way possible. It felt that way for a very long time. It took several delicate months to a year before I could even be around it again. I'd avoid it at every turn. Not have it in my home. Not sitting at the bar area of a restaurant. Not spend time around my hardcore drinking friends. Even now I protect my sobriety like I'm protecting a fragile egg. Fortunately, I've been sober now for over 5 years and I see it for the poison that it is. It was the best but hardest decision I've ever made.

I am an alcoholic. I have conquered it. Most don't.

90% of those who go to rehab relapse.

That doesn't mean how I fought for my sobriety was a great idea. I didn't know at the time I went "cold turkey" to stop drinking that it was very unsafe. It can cause seizures, heart attack, stroke and it can possibly be deadly. AA or a rehab center is much safer but personally the way I did it worked for me.

# **Why do rehabs have such a high relapse rate?**

# Why do rehabs have such a high relapse rate?

**Medications are usually given to the addict to relieve Alcohol Withdrawal Symptoms (AWS).**

Personally, I needed to feel the pain and endure it to never want to go through AWS ever again! Medications mask the pain. If you don't feel the bad side of drinking Alcohol, then all you know is the good side. That feeling you miss when you're drinking will likely creep back up. It makes total sense to me.

**Someone other than the addict has forced the issue and made the addict go to rehab (whether that be the law, a spouse, a relative, anyone other than the addict).**

In my opinion, the addict must make the decisive choice to live a sober life. This is not a decision that can come from anyone else. This is a fight for your life and you're fighting yourself to save yourself!

# My Mottos

# My Mottos

"If you can get sober you can do anything. Nothing will ever be harder than that."

This has been true 100% since choosing to be sober. Through two breakups, several times moving homes and schools to teach, nothing is harder than the fight for your life against Alcohol.

"Nothing is more empowering than turning your flaw into your strength, to say proudly and fearlessly "no thank you" to alcohol feels like I'm wearing a badge of honor."

**Sobriety is that powerful!**

Places and things I used to think I could never go to or do again because "how can I have fun or live my life without Alcohol?" All those crazy concerns fully adjusted and became inconsequential as my body and brain repaired themselves. It just took time. That was my experience. I broke a bone in the middle of my left foot about a year or so before I stopped drinking in a freak electric bike accident. It took six months to heal. I was in a walking boot during the day and a different boot in bed at night. It took months longer to heal than it should have, probably because I was drinking so much Alcohol. The last year of my downward Alcohol spiral, I was feeling tingling, numbness and pain shooting up and down my arms and legs. Within a couple months of being sober, all that went away. I was extremely close to allowing Alcohol to permanently damage me and I didn't realize it. Maybe it was so I can share my story with you? Maybe the purpose is to help someone else who's feeling the anxiety and impending doom that alcohol addicts go through during withdrawals? Just know that it's part of the healing process to take your life back. If it didn't hurt so much, you'd probably go right back to drinking again, right?

## Who can truly understand what you're going through?

## Who can truly understand what you're going through?

Only another person who has experienced alcohol addiction and tackled it can really relate to what you're going through. Your BFF, significant other and your family members are hopefully loving and supportive. Just realize if they haven't experienced alcohol addiction, then they cannot fully understand what you're going through even if they have the best intentions. If they have not gone through it, they cannot fully understand it.

After my mom read my story in its entirety, she had a better understanding of her own alcoholic parents. She was able to forgive them for physical and emotional abuse after realizing the power and control of alcohol addiction.

# Mushy's Role and Legacy

# Mushy's Role and Legacy

About a week after he turned 8-years-old, Mushy hopped over the rainbow bridge and was reunited with his brother, Mr. Chubbles. I could always count on Mushy to give me kisses and show me he loved me. He was loving to everyone who met him. He was a very special bunny. I can't explain the bond I had with Mushy during his 8 years of life. During the most challenging times of my life, he was there loving me. He was my only support when I stopped drinking and without him, I would have been all alone. I stayed at home for weeks when I chose to get sober. As I suffered in bed with the most unbelievable alcohol withdrawals, for weeks this sweet and loving bunny stayed in bed with me. He didn't leave my side. He cuddled with me. He even licked the sweat off me, as I laid there paralyzed in a tremendous amount of pain.

Mushy gave me strength, a purpose, a reason to fight for my life and to fight for him because I was his momma.

**In loving memory of Mushy.**

(Yes, I'm crying as I write this part.)

## The Nots

# The Nots

It is important to not have Alcohol in your home. Not be around it while it still dominates your thoughts. Until you reach a point that you don't think about it all the time, you should protect yourself and your sobriety by not being around it at all. There will be a time in the future when Alcohol becomes your past life and you can live a much better, happier and healthier life without it. Once you feel strong again and know you're the one making the decisions, that's when sobriety becomes powerful, and you know that you're in control! That is when you can be around it with friends and saying "no thank you" feels amazing!

I am someone who understands by my own experiences what an alcoholic goes through during each phase of sobriety.

First is the **Realization Phase**- Wtf I'm an alcoholic and I have a flaw?!?!

Second is the **Decision Phase**- To drink or not to drink? That is the question.

Third is the **Withdrawal Phase**- The fight for your life if you choose to accept it. It's extremely painful but totally worth it!

Fourth is the **Recouperation Phase**- The healing that will take place in your body and brain physically, psychologically, spiritually and emotionally.

Fifth and finally, the **Stability Phase**- You are finally in control of your own life! Alcohol no longer has a hold on you. As Chris Scott would say, you've reached **transcendence**!

None of these phases are easy to choose or go through.

If you are suffering with alcoholism, substance abuse or just need someone to talk to and understand what you're going through, I want you to know you can always reach out to me. It's very important to know you have someone who cares about you and understands what you're going through. I will always be one of those people. I make a great listener if you need to vent. I will be your cheerleader if you decide to make positive changes in your life. I will always keep anything you tell me confidential. I just want to help other people who are struggling with alcohol addiction. I wish at the time I went "cold turkey" that I had a friend who was there for me.

You are not alone.

If you need more advice or someone on your side, my email is TWDConfessions@outlook.com

# Spiritual Messages

# Spiritual Message 1

Become all God created you to be.

Come back to a place of peace.

The gracious hand of God is in our lives.

Live inspired.

Reach your dreams.

## Spiritual Message 2 ~ By Author John Roedel

Me: Hey God.
God: Hello.....
Me: I'm falling apart. Can you put me back together?
God: I would rather not.
Me: Why?
God: Because you aren't a puzzle.
Me: What about all the pieces of my life that are falling down onto the ground?
God: Let them stay there for a while. They fell off for a reason. Take some time and decide if you need any of those pieces back.
Me: You don't understand! I'm breaking down!
God: No - you don't understand. You are breaking through. What you are feeling are just growing pains. You are shedding the things and the people in your life that are holding you back. You aren't falling apart. You are falling into place. Relax. Take some deep breaths and allow those things you don't need any more to fall off of you. Quit holding onto the pieces that don't fit you anymore. Let them fall off. Let them go.
Me: Once I start doing that, what will be left of me?
God: Only the very best pieces of you.
Me: I'm scared of changing.
God: I keep telling you - YOU AREN'T CHANGING!! YOU ARE BECOMING!
Me: Becoming who?
God: Becoming who I created you to be! A person of light and love and charity and hope and courage and joy and mercy and grace and compassion. I made you for more than the shallow pieces you have decided to adorn yourself with that you cling to with such greed and fear. Let those things fall off of you. I love you! Don't change! ... Become! Become! Become who I made you to be. I'm going to keep telling you this until you remember it.
Me: There goes another piece.
God: Yep. Let it be.
Me: So ... I'm not broken?
God: Of course Not! - but you are breaking like the dawn. It's a new day. Become!!!

# Drinking Vocabulary Glossary

# Drinking Vocabulary Glossary

It may seem strange but to fully understand where you or your loved one falls into the realm of safe or unsafe drinking, I'm introducing these definitions to you.

**The Alcohol Consumer/ Are you drinking too much?**
**Let's Find Out.**

## Drinking in moderation:

**For women:** 1 drink or less per day
**For men:** 2 drinks or less per day

**Alcohol misuse:**

**For women:** 3 drinks or more per day **OR** more than 7 drinks per week
**For men:** 4 drinks or more per day **OR** more than 14 drinks per week

**Binge drinking:**

**For women:** More than 4 drinks over 2 hours
**For men:** More than 5 drinks over 2 hours

FYI- For someone addicted to Alcohol, the number of drinks mentioned above is **nothing**!

That's how strong and serious alcohol addiction becomes…

**Alcohol Use Disorder (AUD):** is also known as alcohol misuse, alcohol dependence, alcohol addiction, and alcoholism.

**High-Functioning Alcoholic (HFA):** is a person who maintains their job and relationships, managing to fulfill their professional and personal responsibilities while consistently drinking alcohol at high tolerance levels.

**GABA:** (Gamma-aminobutyric acid) this is the brain's main inhibitory chemical. This causes a temporary relief from anxiety and a sense of calmness while drinking alcohol.

It acts as an inhibitory neurotransmitter, meaning it helps to regulate and calm brain activity. GABA plays a crucial role in reducing anxiety, promoting relaxation, and maintaining mental well-being. It binds to specific receptors in the brain, known as GABA receptors, to produce its calming effects.

**Glutamate:** The brain's main excitatory chemical. Alcohol suppresses your "fight or flight" response and ability to respond to danger and leads to a slowdown in brain activity.

Glutamate normally increases brain activity and energy levels by acting as an excitatory neurotransmitter. It facilitates communication between neurons and is essential for various cognitive processes.

Though there are many other neurotransmitters that effect brain chemistry while drinking alcohol (Dopamine and Serotonin, for example) we will only explore Gaba and Glutamate.

Drinking alcohol changes the GABA receptors and Glutamate receptors causing a slowdown of brain functionality, give a feeling of decreased anxiety and sedation (usually people fall asleep easily). We can also make stupid decisions with this slowdown of brain functionality. (Hint. Hint.)

**Tolerance:** The brain reacts to alcohol by decreasing GABA and increasing Glutamate. The more alcohol you drink over time, the more alcohol you will need to continue to achieve that feeling of alcohol you think you enjoy. It's become your new normal. If you've gotten to this point, please stop drinking.

**Delirium Tremens (DTs):** Occur 2 – 3 days to a week post drinking for those who are misusing alcohol and/or binge drinking alcohol. This is a severe form of alcohol withdrawal that can cause heart attack, stroke and/or death. More information about DTs is below in Stage 4.

**Kindling:** Each time an alcoholic becomes sober and then relapses, it is harder for the body and brain to get sober again. Every time this process is repeated alcohol withdrawal symptoms will be even more traumatic.

**Alcohol Withdrawal Symptoms (AWS):** Severity of AWS will be due to the various changes in brain chemistry activity caused by prolonged and excessive alcohol use. As alcohol leaves the body, in the first couple hours the body starts to go into "fight or flight" mode.

Below is an example of how alcohol withdrawal symptoms progress in the body, causing physiological, behavioral, gastrointestinal and mood changes.

**Stage 1: 6-12 hours post drinking**. Symptoms include shaking, sweating, extreme anxiety, body pains, numbness/tingling in the arms and legs, headache, insomnia, nervousness, restless, nausea, and abdominal pain.

**Stage 2: 12-24 hours post drinking.** Symptoms include (all or the above and) inability to eat, diarrhea, vomiting, high blood pressure, irritability, increased body temperature, fast heart rate, rapid/abnormal breathing and confusion.

**Stage 3: 1-2 days post drinking.** Symptoms include (all or the above and) agitation, tremors, feeling disoriented, fatigued, hyperthermia, cold sweats, feeling of extreme horror, nightmares, hallucinations, fever and seizures.

**Stage 4: 2 days – a week post drinking.** Symptoms include (all or the above and) delirium tremens (DTs), which is a severe form of withdrawal symptoms that can cause severe confusion, agitation, excessive sweating, inability to think clearly, extreme hyperactivity, dehydration, hallucinations, heart attack, stroke and/or death.

Thank you for reading my miraculous story of recovery and I hope you found it helpful.

In Loving Memory of Mr. Chubbles and Mushy.

## Now, For The Fun Part!

Time for some pictures of their bunny love…

Mr. Chubbles (left) and Mushy (right) In My School Garden

Mr. Chubbles, Mushy and Momma

Mr. Chubbles Kissing Mushy

Mr. Chubbles and Momma

Mushy Love

Momma Kissing Mushy

Mushy Kissing Momma

Mushy's Ride to School

Mushy with his Lion Rug

Mushy Napping with his Pre-K Friend!

## Bunny Art Photos

Mr. Chubbles

Mushy

## Praise for the Author

*Hi Tiffany! I finally had a chance to read your book and it's amazing!!! I'm moved by your words about me and Fit Recovery - it was just a piece of the puzzle for you, although I'm so glad to hear that it was a meaningful one.*

*I'm so happy for you - keep up the great work!*

*~ Chris Scott ~*

*Creator of www.fitrecovery.com and Author of the book "Drinking Sucks!"*

TDWConfessions@outlook.com

If you want advice or support on your journey to recovery, please reach out to me.

**You're not alone.**

*Tiffany*

Made in the USA
Las Vegas, NV
08 March 2026

43237518R00056